As far as we can discern,
the sole purpose of human existence is to kindle a light
in the darkness of mere being.

C. G. Jung, *Memories, Dreams, Reflections*

VIEW OF COLLINGWOOD
Collingwood

TRAILS OF LIGHT

PHOTOGRAPHS OF A CANADIAN BIOSPHERE
ঔঔ THE BRUCE TRAIL ঔঔ

THERESA KAZMIERCZAK-STUBLER

VIKING

VIKING
Published by the Penguin Group
Penguin Books Canada Ltd, 10 Alcorn Avenue, Toronto, Ontario, Canada M4V 3B2
Penguin Books Ltd, 27 Wrights Lane, London W8 5TZ, England
Viking Penguin, a division of Penguin Books USA Inc., 375 Hudson Street, New York, New York 10014, U.S.A.
Penguin Books Australia Ltd, Ringwood, Victoria, Australia
Penguin Books (NZ) Ltd, 182-190 Wairau Road, Auckland 10, New Zealand

Penguin Books Ltd, Registered Offices: Harmondsworth, Middlesex, England

First published 1992

10 9 8 7 6 5 4 3 2 1
Copyright © Theresa Kazmierczak-Stubler, 1992

Printed and bound in Canada on re-cycled acid free paper ∞

Canadian Cataloguing in Publication Data

    Kazmierczak-Stubler, Theresa, 1954–
        Trails of light

    ISBN 0-670-84853-0

    1. Bruce Trail (Ont.) - Pictorial works.
    I. Title.

    FC3093.4.K39 1992   917.13   C92-094516-3
    F1059.B78K39 1992

To Rich,
the energy behind *Trails of Light*.

ACKNOWLEDGEMENTS

After looking through many wonderful books and ignoring the acknowledgements, I find myself in the ironic position of writing some myself. Now I understand the importance of this page. It is a small attempt to thank some of the people who have helped and inspired me.

The first of those people are two of the masters of photography, Ansel Adams and Edward Weston. I never met Ansel Adams; however, his wonderful books, *The Camera*, *The Negative*, and *The Print*, continue to be unequalled sources of information and ideas for me. Edward Weston's high-contrast prints are a constant inspiration; they seem to scale down the largest of subjects to a bare few, visually stunning details.

John Sexton taught me how to use large-format cameras, helped me understand the zone system, and shared many of his darkroom techniques — all this in an all-too-brief two-week workshop. I mostly thank John for instilling in me the art of experimentation in the darkroom, and for his style of teaching: learning by doing. I hope that, someday, my work can be shown side-by-side with his.

I owe a special thanks to Tom Beckett of Beckett Gallery in Hamilton, who believed enough in me to produce a show of my work when I was in the beginning stages. This, from an experienced photographer, helped me to believe in myself.

There are others to whom I extend my thanks:

To Deborah Siksay, for the many nights in small motels on the northern part of the trail. Deb carried my pack, because of my injury, and we shared great conversations and a lot of laughter;

To Michael Intrator of Blackbox Printing, Chicago, for his continued interest in my career. His many helpful suggestions have been noted and appreciated;

To Penguin Books Canada, for believing enough in my work (with the minimum of facts) to agree to publish it and accept the book as I envisioned it;

To Ernie Herzig of Herzig Somerville in Toronto. Years ago he was the first to publish two of my prints as posters. Now he has agreed to print this book using his special talents and his love of the arts;

To Robert Bateman, for taking the time from his busy schedule to write a bit of philosophy for this book. The world needs more people like Robert, people who are willing to give something back to what they believe in;

To Andrew Smith, the designer, for understanding that this is a book of fine art photographs, not a touristy trail book. I appreciate his expertise and sensitivity;

To Kodak Canada, for providing the paper and chemicals so that I could complete the original prints;

And, finally, to the many therapists I have had in the last four years who kept — and are keeping — my body going as much as possible. The accident, which almost took away my desire to be a photographer, because of the constant pain, was nullified by these special people. Without them, I would not have endured.

TRAILS OF LIGHT

CONTENTS

PROTECTING THE WILDERNESS

ROBERT BATEMAN

In the early 1960s, North America was a different world. We had just experienced the biggest economic growth in the history of the planet, but some of us were starting to wonder. For centuries, humankind in much of the world has been in continual pursuit of power and convenience. Thirty years ago, for the first time in history, thinking people were becoming sceptical that this could go on forever. They were showing others how ancient modes of transportation, like walking, could have value in themselves: the Kennedys were thinking of Camelot, and many people were taking a hard look at the overwhelming of nature by the forces of development. A valiant few were turning towards hiking and canoeing, even though they could afford fast cars and power boats.

With this desire for physical exercise in nature, away from the noise of machines, along with the growing awareness to protect the vanishing wilderness, "Use It or Lose It" became a slogan among conservationists. One of the great accomplishments of a recent era had been the creation of the Appalachian Trail.

During these years, I was an active member in a number of naturalists' clubs and was excited to see the swelling interest in the enjoyment and protection of nature. Ray Lowes and I were on the executive of the Hamilton Naturalist Club. I can remember one moment as if it were yesterday. We were at an executive meeting in someone's living room and we happened to be sitting next to each other on the couch. During a dull part, probably a financial report, Ray turned to me and whispered, "What do you think of the idea of a walking trail along the Niagara Escarpment — something like the Appalachian Trail?"

I immediately responded, "A great idea!" and after a moment's reflection added, "But who would do it?"

Ray retorted, "If we talk that way, nothing will ever get done. Let's just do it!"

"Right you are," I agreed. The rest, I'm happy to say, is history.

Ray Lowes is the one who carried the ball, but a unique combination of historical factors had made it possible. The pioneers had cleared the easy parts of Upper Canada, such as the Peel Plain, and skipped over the rough and rocky Escarpment. They had left a natural, relatively unspoiled ribbon between the most affluent and densely populated parts of Ontario.

The midset of the 1960s was ripe for a conservation elite to move the general public toward this worthy project. The idea of the Bruce Trail, at the beginning, was like motherhood and apple pie. But in the last 25 years, it has changed the map of Ontario, influenced the awareness of Canadians, and has brought — and will continue to bring — countless hours of pleasure to millions.

Robert Bateman is one of Canada's best-known artists and an eminent naturalist and environmentalist. Living in southern Ontario for most of his life, he has been a leader in promoting the importance of the natural world surrounding us. Among his many contributions, Bateman was one of the founding members of the Bruce Trail Association, and served for many years on the Niagara Escarpment Commission. He now makes his home with his family in the Gulf Islands, B.C.

IMAGES OF ELEGANCE AND ECONOMY

THERESA KAZMIERCZAK-STUBLER AND THE BRUCE TRAIL PHOTOGRAPHS

JAMES G. ALINDER

Theresa Kazmierczak-Stubler is a photographer with a strong vision. Her images are composed with elegance and economy. Viewed individually, each photograph is a precise expression; together, this collection forms an aesthetic document of the Bruce Trail and its surrounding environment, the Niagara Escarpment.

In 1984, Kazmierczak-Stubler left her employment as manager of a Toronto-area boutique to pursue her interest in photography full-time. She studied the medium avidly, progressing from enthusiastic amateur to competent professional. Among the books she read during those years were *The Camera*, *The Negative* and *The Print*, Ansel Adams's technical series on fine photography. The influence of Adams's teaching is evident in the technical prowess of the images reproduced in this book.

In 1987, Kazmierczak-Stubler attended a workshop given by John Sexton, Ansel Adams's former assistant and a photographer of tremendous ability. Sexton taught her the zone system, a photographic technique devised by Adams wherein the range of tones that can be produced in a black and white photograph is divided into eleven zones, with pitch-black at zone 0 and pure white at zone 10. With this system of applied sensitometry, she gained the ability to assess the general contrast range of her subject and to determine what specific areas related to specific zones of tone in the final print. This enabled her to expose and develop the film according to learned standards that provide the desired densities for the visualized image.

The experience inspired Kazmierczak-Stubler: she described the workshop as a "great awakening," and committed herself to taking her photography as far as she could. She purchased a 4 x 5 camera and rebuilt her darkroom to accommodate her newly acquired skills.

In 1988, her photography career began to take off. Mintmark Press contracted to produce and distribute two posters of her images. The Beckett Gallery of Hamilton, one of Canada's finest galleries, planned an exhibition of her work. Two weeks before the Beckett show, Kazmierczak-Stubler's fortunes reversed. She was involved in a serious auto crash in which she suffered a debilitating back injury. The accident and the time spent recuperating kept her out of the darkroom and put her photography on hold.

Kazmierczak-Stubler surmounted these difficulties and began to photograph again in earnest. In 1989, she organized her own one-person exhibition in Dundas, Ontario. The display included photographs of the Bruce Trail, and the response to these images was very favourable. It was during this show that she decided to do a book on the Bruce Trail. Her home was on the trail, near its southern terminus, so certain areas of her subject would be close. But given its length, over 700 kilometres, photographing the entire trail would require months of effort.

Still hampered by her injury, she hired an assistant to help carry her photographic equipment. Kazmierczak-Stubler refused to succumb to the challenges or her injury. The resulting photographs reveal the patience and persistence of a confident artist.

Among the most compelling of the images reproduced here is "Top of Tews Falls." After photographing the falls in all seasons and from many different vantage points, Kazmierczak-Stubler found the optimum light one late-fall morning. The trees are nearly bare, and the sky is overcast. Still, the landscape is depicted sensitively and sympathetically: we see a place of quiet beauty, stark and placid. The geological strata behind the falls speak of the passage of time and testify to the creation of the Escarpment, formed by a fracturing of the earth's crust. The kinetic vertical of the falls contrasts with the solid horizontal strata. As winter approaches, the flow has diminished to near translucence, enabling the viewer to see the strata behind the falls. The strands of water, the strata and the tree trunks all seem to have a nearly uniform thickness. Except for the largest tree, which stands perfectly upright, the trees above the falls tilt slightly to the left, bent by years of wind. The split-rail fence alone reveals the human hand, but there is no sense of intrusion — the presence is entirely harmonious.

"Bloom" suggests the influence of Imogen Cunningham, a California photographer who worked extensively with flowers. As in Cunningham's images, the petals here are clear, distinct and sharply delineated. The flower seems to unfold in layers, offering its innermost beauty to the viewer. The dark background emphasizes the lighter tones of the petals, drawing the viewer's eye to the centre of the flower, the lightest part of the image. The bloom shows some signs of decay: the tips of the petals have begun to wither and wrinkle. Behind the flower, however, the viewer may discern a bud that seems on the verge of opening. Thus, Kazmierczak-Stubler subtly alludes to nature's cycles of death and renewal.

As suggested by the presence of the fence in "Top of Tews Falls," Kazmierczak-Stubler has not limited her vision to the rugged natural glory of the Niagara Escarpment. She also turns her camera to man-made structures along the trail, revealing their relationship with the natural environment. Several of these images show nature reclaiming space once occupied by humans. In the foreground of "Barn," for example, we see a silo that has been destroyed by the elements, twisted into a nearly unrecognizable form. As photographed by Kazmierczak-Stubler, the remains of the silo bear more resemblance to a natural form — a tangled copse of trees, a windblown haystack — than they do to the original silo. The viewer is left to wonder how long the barn will last before it meets the fate of its neighbour.

The boathouse in "Little Tub Harbour" seems on the verge of collapse. The thick cable, two feet below the roof-line, suggests a last-ditch effort to hold the structure together. It is apparent, however, that cable or no, the boathouse will inevitably decline, soon to be no more than a pile of boards at the water's edge.

The dilapidated building is not portrayed as evidence of nature's pitiless victory over the forces of human beings — quite the contrary. In Kazmierczak-Stubler's photographs, nature is patient and serene, more a witness to our ephemeral presence than a wilful destroyer. Nor does Kazmierczak-Stubler show the presence of humans as a gross invasion on sacred Nature: the boathouse is portrayed as tenderly as its surroundings. The painted sailboats on the door evoke nostalgia, a sense of loss of times past. The conflict of human effort and nature is not shown as a violent clash, but rather a constant and steady process, wherein our efforts are humbled by enduring nature.

The only conclusion one can draw is that we must endeavour to create structures that will be in harmony with nature. In "Stone Hut" we see such a structure. The hut is doubly concealed —— first by overarching trees and second by new-fallen snow. This concealment brings to mind the lost cabins in folk and fairy tales, lending the image an air of mystery. Unlike the structures in "Barn" and "Little Tub Harbour," the stone hut seems in no danger of collapse. The rigors of nature along the Niagara Escarpment place several imperatives on those who would build there: their constructions must be solid, secluded and unobtrusive, values embodied by the stone hut. The stone hut will last, but the glory of the photograph is all nature's. The pattern of the snow on the trees is complex and engaging, a testament to the unfathomable beauty of chance.

Similarly, the criss-crossing branches of "Devil's Glen" create a beguiling interplay of light and shadow. The trees give the photograph a strong vertical presence, in contrast to the much thinner horizontal branches. But the filtered sun creates highlights on the branches, making the horizontal lines more interesting to the eye than the massive, vertical lines of the trees. This dynamic interaction of lines speaks to Stubler's abilities of perception.

The stairway in the photograph again reveals the presence of human beings. The steps are constructed of wood, suggesting an effort to co-exist with the forest rather than to disturb it, and, indeed, the stairway seems utterly at peace in its environment. Like the stone hut, the stairway leading to the forest is slightly mysterious. The image reminds the viewer that contact with nature is, quite literally, rejuvenating. We need only step into the forest to be young again, transported to a place of intrigue and fantasy.

I suspect that this aspect of hiking the trail has been crucial to Kazmierczak-Stubler's recovery from her injury. Perhaps that misfortune enabled her to capture some of the recreative powers of nature in her photographs. She has already decided on her next project: a book on the Banff-to-Jasper area of the Canadian Rockies. The results, I predict, will be as successful as her images are here.

James G. Alinder is the author or editor of over two dozen photography books. He served for more than a decade as the executive director of The Friends of Photography and was instrumental in creating its Ansel Adams Center in San Francisco.

THE BRUCE TRAIL

AN ECOLOGICAL TREASURE

DOUGLAS J. ROBERTSON

For more than a quarter-century, the Bruce Trail — a popular footpath along southern Ontario's scenic Niagara Escarpment — has been enjoyed by countless hikers and nature lovers.

The story of the trail's origins is worth telling, but to do so means looking first at the Escarpment, for these two elements — the trail and the Escarpment — are inextricably linked.

From the time of the earliest settlements, the Escarpment's high dolostone cliffs, shallow rocky soils, waterfalls, and other characteristics have molded human land-use activities. For native peoples, the region provided many good hunting grounds and settlement sites. For European settlers, the Escarpment presented both problems and benefits: the land was less than ideal for agriculture, and its topography was a barrier to road and railway construction; however, swift-flowing streams and waterfalls provided power, the basis for many industrial settlements in the early and mid-19th century. Then, as steam power and, later, hydro electricity stimulated growth away from the Escarpment, the old mill-towns declined.

After the initial periods of lumbering, new-growth forests remained generally undisturbed, and many areas of the Escarpment became natural oases — islands of original flora, fauna, and scenery.

With the building boom that followed World War II, many of these oases came under pressure as well. The accelerating growth of Ontario's major urban centres fuelled a seemingly insatiable demand for the Escarpment's aggregate resources, gravel and crushed stone. Urban growth itself was spreading into the area, and by the 1960s it was clear to some concerned Ontarians that this last remnant of original landscape was threatened and would soon be lost forever.

Among this group was Raymond N. Lowes, a Hamilton naturalist and metallurgist with Stelco. A native of Saskatchewan, where distant horizons were the only limits to boyhood rambling, his view of the steady assault of the Escarpment was particularly acute. But what could be done?

After many discussions between Ray and fellow members in the Hamilton Naturalists' Club and the Federation of Ontario Naturalists, the seed of an idea germinated: build a nature trail, over 700 kilometres of footpath from Queenston to Tobermory, so that people could experience first-hand the many unique natural treasures along the Niagara Escarpment. It was also hoped that the building of such a trail would draw public attention to the need to protect this significant part of Ontario's natural heritage.

The Escarpment, a massive ridge of shale, sandstone and dolostone, is the eroded remains of the uplifted and warped rim of an ancient sea. Organic material from this sea accumulated over millions of years along with deposits of thick layers of sediment from the rivers that flowed into it. These structures and the fossil remains are a paradise for geologists. Erosion by rivers has produced spectacular features along the trail, such as the Niagara Gorge, the Beaver Valley, and Devil's Glen.

On September 23, 1960, the first step in a noble venture was taken by Ray Lowes, Norman Pearson, Philip Gosling, and Dr. Robert MacLaren. Armed with little more than some topographical maps and a lot of enthusiasm, these four "founding fathers" began planning the Bruce Trail, so named because it was to be a trail to the Bruce Peninsula. The name also honours James Bruce, the 8th Earl of Elgin and Governor General of Canada from 1847 to 1854.

In the ensuing months, this small core of original Bruce trailers steadily grew as more and more people recognized the

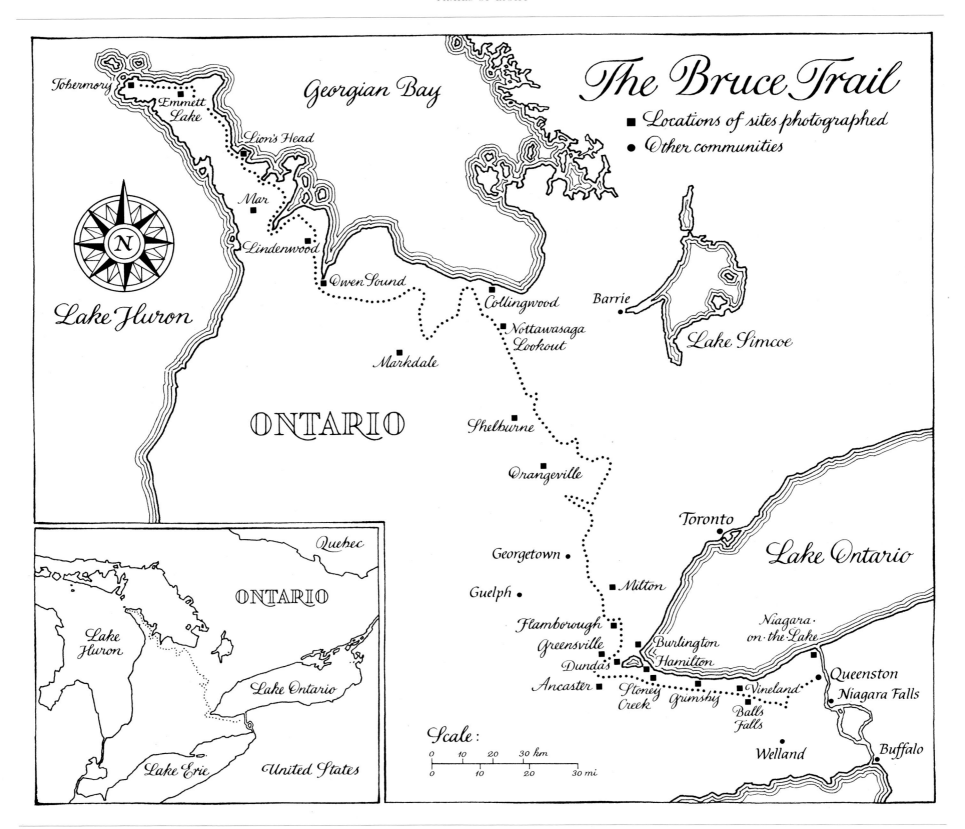

The Bruce Trail

■ Locations of sites photographed
● Other communities

Georgian Bay

Tobermory
Emmett Lake
Lion's Head
Mar
Lindenwood
Owen Sound
Collingwood
Barrie
Lake Simcoe
Nottawasaga Lookout
Markdale

Lake Huron

ONTARIO

Shelburne

Orangeville

Toronto

Lake Ontario

Georgetown

Guelph

Milton

Flamborough
Greensville
Dundas
Ancaster
Stoney Creek
Grimsby
Vineland
Balls Falls
Burlington
Hamilton
Niagara on-the-Lake
Queenston
Niagara Falls
Welland
Buffalo

Quebec

ONTARIO

Lake Huron

Lake Ontario

Lake Erie

United States

Scale :
0 10 20 30 km
0 10 20 30 mi

fundamental soundness of the new idea and lent their support. By March 13, 1963, the fledgling Bruce Trail Association was ready for incorporation under Ontario Letters Patent, and on October 15 that same year, the Association held its first Annual General Meeting.

Parallel to this organizational growth, work on the Bruce Trail itself was also well underway. Volunteers talked with hundreds of landowners along the mapped route, negotiating trail access agreements, sealed with no more than a handshake. Other workers cut trail through the bush and along fence-rows, painting the now-famous white blazes to mark the route, erecting signs and building stiles and footbridges.

In less than seven years all was ready, and on June 10, 1967, Canada's Centennial trail was officially opened.

The next decade was one of growth. Membership grew from 60 to 7,500, local Bruce Trail Clubs were created, more campsites were added to the growing range of trail resources, and ever- increasing numbers of people, from around the world as well as from southern Ontario, discovered the joys of exploring the Niagara Escarpment on foot.

Little remains of pre-European southern Ontario, and what does can often only be found along the trail, including 40 species of orchids and 50 species of ferns. For birdwatchers, more than 300 species inhabit or fly through this area. During a recent spring migration, members of one club counted over 3,000 Red-tailed Hawks, 17 Bald Eagles, 8 Golden Eagles, 46 Osprey and nearly 4,000 Sharp-shinned Hawks.

For history buffs, there is a legion of sites: remnants from the War of 1812-14, Welland canals (there were four!), early Loyalists' settlements, old mill sites, and castles.

Parts of the trail challenge experienced hikers; other stretches provide a comfortable outing for families with small children. And anyone with an interest in history, geology, or biology has a feast of offerings. Names along the trail only hint at the diversity: Beaver Shelter, Bruce's Caves, Devil's Punchbowl, Overhanging Point, Slough of Despond, Tiffany Falls, and Whippoorwill Bay.

Today, the Bruce Trail has become acknowledged as an important recreational resource, not only by hikers but by neighbouring landowners and others who live near the trail, by local Chambers of Commerce, tourist associations, municipal councils, and numerous provincial and federal government agencies. The trail is recognized as a significant part of the Niagara Escarpment, which, in 1990, was designated a UNESCO World Biosphere Reserve, giving international recognition to the extraordinary qualities that Bruce Trail members have always known it possessed. This put it in the company of the Galapagos Islands and Africa's Serengeti National Park as an ecologically important area with unique natural features.

The Bruce Trail is a testament to the dedicated individuals who turned a dream into a reality. The world is indeed a better place for their efforts.

Douglas J. Robertson, a member of the Bruce Trail Association since 1967, served as Executive Director of the Association from 1980 to 1991. He is now the Senior Environmental Planner for Conestoga-Rovers, an environmental engineering consulting firm located in Waterloo, Ontario. He has walked the Bruce Trail from end to end, some parts many times over.

MEMORY AND DISCOVERY

THERESA KAZMIERCZAK-STUBLER

I grew up near the Bruce Trail, so there are parts of it I have known most of my life — swimming, fishing, and sharing picnics. There are also sections and sites I have not yet seen. I could spend a lifetime photographing this wonderful Escarpment and never really know it.

There's always a choice — or a tug — between familiar places and undiscovered paths. One brings associations, through memory; the other means risks and awakenings. Sometimes you need the comfort of childhood surroundings, and there are times when it's important to take chances, to test your limits. What I choose to photograph depends on what is happening in my life, on my intuition. I also depend on my trusty notebook, filled with locations visited in the past, but when either the light or the season wasn't quite right. Those are the things I pay attention to.

With my photography, I want control, or as much as I can get. There are enough variables: light, shadows, weather, time of day, season — to say nothing of storms, insects, poison ivy, twisted ankles and frost-bitten fingers — let alone my physical limitations. That's why I work mostly in black and white. I load my own cassettes and loaders, develop my own film with different formulas, and print, matte and frame my own work. When the negative is in the enlarger, I have that chance to look again, because the negative and the print look so different. I can make fine or large adjustments, develop or print for this or that quality. Working with black and white offers many possibilities, and I still can get results that look like the photo I took, the image I saw through the lens.

Before my auto accident in 1988, I could carry a 60-pound back-pack plus my cameras and tripod. To say that my life has changed would be an understatement. But with the help and encouragement of my husband, and my commitment to this project, I made adjustments, knowing that the results would give me a sense of accomplishment. I confess that I'm not a "morning" person, even though I know the early hours bring remarkable light; however, with "Stone Hut" I did get up at 5 a.m. to photograph it before anyone had a chance to leave footprints. The light at dusk is different, but equally exciting. That's my time of day. That's when I really "see" things.

I'm a private person; I'm not keen on crowds; I don't even shoot "big" landscapes that much. I tend to be selective, to look for the detail, the pattern, the structure. Photography takes patience. Setting up a large-format camera takes time. And I have to wait for the light, the right moment. It may not come, or I may get lucky. When I was getting ready for "Wall of Ivy," the leaves were suddenly hit with the right light. And so the result is far different than the image I thought I would capture, and much better.

Some of the things I photographed are no longer there. That gives me such a sense of how transient human effort is. Even the railway tracks are gone. In "Birch Trees," I saw the initials carved into the trunks; I don't avoid the marks of humans in nature; I only lament our arrogance.

But I am excited about the interest and participation that we are showing in restoring and preserving of the environment. These endeavours are not a fad. Our eyes have been opened. While taking these photographs, I met many people: some who walk the trail frequently, many first-time visitors, a few from different countries. Everyone has been so grateful that a haven like this is ours to enjoy, and they were delighted with the well-maintained trails.

My years in photography have shown me how nature has provided for our enjoyment and survival. But, for too many years our excuses have come too easily. Our resources have seemed too abundant to conserve, recycle, reuse or restore — and at what a cost! Now, we know they are too precious not to protect.

Doing our part to preserve our environment surely yields the same kind of excitement as hikers share, the same rewards and enthusiasm. And these qualities have such a magic way of spreading.

TRAILS OF LIGHT

THE PLATES

TRAIN TRACKS
Dundas Conservation Area

FEATHER
Stoney Creek Battlefield

WINTER
Websters Falls, Greensville

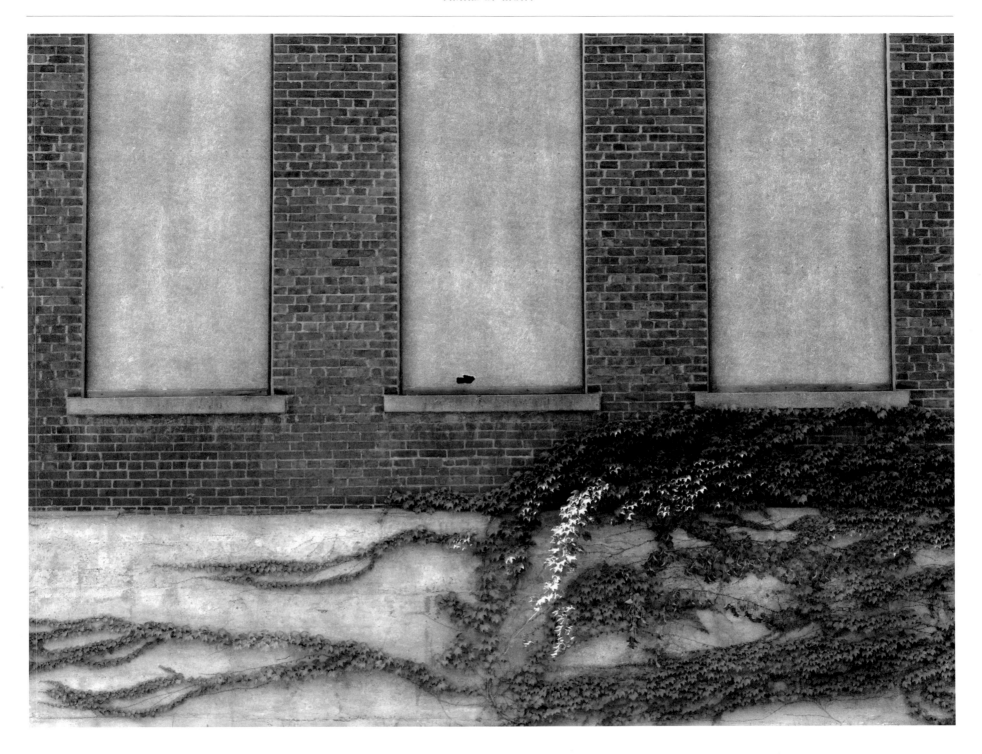

WALL OF IVY
Dundas

ROOTS
Mount Nemo Conservation Area, Burlington

GRIST MILL
Balls Falls, Vineland

BIRCH TREES
Websters Falls, Greensville

WAGON WHEEL
Orangeville

BLOOM
Nottawasaga Lookout

WEBSTERS FALLS
Greensville

BARN
Hwy # 6, North of Mar

MARE & COLT
Greensville

TINY FLOWERS
Milton

TREE IN BLOSSOM
Royal Botanical Gardens, Dundas

LITTLE TUB HARBOUR
Tobermory

SNAIL
Beaver Valley, Markdale

TREE
Hamilton

TIFFANY FALLS
Ancaster

BOATS
Kelso Beach, Owen Sound

Roots & Rocks
Inglis Falls, Owen Sound

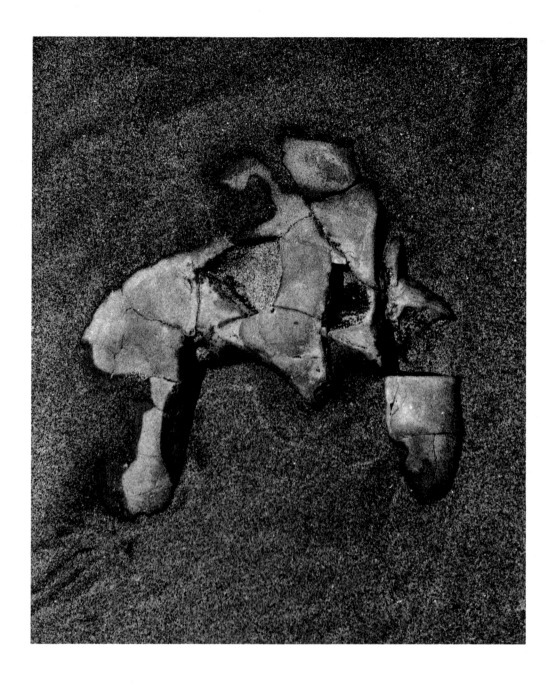

STONE IN SAND
Lion's Head

IVY-COVERED POLE
Flamborough

MILKWEED PODS
Dundas Valley Conservation Area

MOON ECLIPSE
From Dundas Peak

THE POINT
Sassafras Point, Cootes Paradise, Hamilton

WASHINGTON PROFILE
Collingwood Caves, Collingwood

CANADA GOOSE & GOSLING
Bass Lake, Lindenwood

UPPER POND AT TEWS FALLS
Greensville

TOP OF TEWS FALLS
Greensville

FOOT OF TEWS FALLS
Greensville

BIG TUB HARBOUR
Tobermory

Grapes
Vineland

QUEENSTON HEIGHTS
Niagara-on-the-Lake

Flight
Emmett Lake, Bruce Peninsula National Park

TREES
Beamer Memorial Conservation Area, Grimsby

SIMCOE
Fort George, Niagara-on-the-Lake

Devil's Glen
Devil's Glen Provincial Park, Collingwood

DUCK
Boyne Valley Provincial Park, Shelburne

BULRUSHES
Cootes Paradise, Hamilton

STONE HUT
Websters Falls, Greensville

LEAVES ON MOSS
Bruce's Caves Conservation Area, Collingwood

LIST OF PLATES

Plate	Title	Format	Date Taken	Original Print Size	Location
1	View of Collingwood	4 x 5	Sept. '89	14 x 11	Collingwood
2	Train Tracks	4 x 5	Oct. '89	11 x 14	Dundas Conservation Area
3	Feather	4 x 5	Oct. '89	8 x 9¾	Stoney Creek Battlefield
4	Winter	4 x 5	Jan. '88	11 x 14	Websters Falls, Greensville
5	Wall of Ivy	4 x 5	Aug. '87	14 x 11	Dundas
6	Roots	4 x 5	Aug. '87	8 x 10	Mount Nemo Conservation Area, Burlington
7	Grist Mill	4 x 5	Oct. '89	14 x 11	Balls Falls, Vineland
8	Birch Trees	4 x 5	Oct. '89	11 x 14	Websters Falls, Greensville
9	Wagon Wheel	4 x 5	Oct. '89	11 x 14	Orangeville
10	Bloom	4 x 5	Aug. '89	8 x 6½	Nottawasaga Lookout
11	Websters Falls	4 x 5	Oct. '87	11 x 14	Greensville
12	Barn	4 x 5	Sept. '89	14 x 11	Hwy # 6, North of Mar
13	Mare & Colt	4 x 5	May '88	14 x 11	Greensville
14	Tiny Flowers	4 x 5	May '88	11 x 14	Milton
15	Tree in Blossom	4 x 5	Apr. '91	14 x 11	Royal Botanical Gardens, Dundas
16	Little Tub Harbour	4 x 5	Sept. '89	14 x 11	Tobermory
17	Snail	4 x 5	Oct. '89	11 x 14	Beaver Valley, Markdale
18	Tree	4 x 5	Aug. '87	7 x 12¼	Hamilton
19	Tiffany Falls	4 x 5	Oct. '91	11 x 14	Ancaster
20	Boats	4 x 5	Sept. '89	14 x 11	Kelso Beach, Owen Sound
21	Roots & Rocks	4 x 5	Sept. '89	14 x 11	Inglis Falls, Owen Sound

Plate	Title	Format	Date Taken	Original Print Size	Location
22	Stone in Sand	35mm	Apr. '89	8 x 10	Lion's Head
23	Ivy-Covered Pole	4 x 5	Oct. '88	11 x 14	Flamborough
24	Milkweed Pods	4 x 5	Oct. '90	10 x 8	Dundas Valley Conservation Area
25	Moon Eclipse	4 x 5	Aug. '89	20 x 16	From Dundas Peak
26	The Point	4 x 5	Oct. '91	9 x 10½	Sassafras Point, Cootes Paradise, Hamilton
27	Washington Profile	4 x 5	Sept. '89	10 x 13	Collingwood Caves, Collingwood
28	Canada Goose & Gosling	35mm	May '86	14 x 11	Bass Lake, Lindenwood
29	Upper Pond at Tews Falls	4 x 5	Oct. '89	14 x 11	Greensville
30	Top of Tews Falls	4 x 5	Nov. '89	11 x 14	Greensville
31	Foot of Tews Falls	4 x 5	Oct. '89	11 x 14	Greensville
32	Big Tub Harbour	4 x 5	Sept. '89	11 x 14	Tobermory
33	Grapes	4 x 5	Oct. '89	11½ x 8½	Vineland
34	Queenston Heights	4 x 5	Apr. '91	11½ x 9	Niagara-on-the-Lake
35	Flight	35mm	May '89	10¾ x 7	Emmett Lake, Bruce Peninsula National Park
36	Trees	4 x 5	Apr. '91	14 x 11	Beamer Memorial Conservation Area, Grimsby
37	Simcoe	4 x 5	Apr. '91	7½ x 9½	Fort George, Niagara-on-the-Lake
38	Devil's Glen	4 x 5	Oct. '89	11 x 14	Devil's Glen Provincial Park, Collingwood
39	Duck	4 x 5	Oct. '87	8 x 10	Boyne Valley Provincial Park, Shelburne
40	Bulrushes	4 x 5	Nov. '89	14 x 11	Cootes Paradise, Hamilton
41	Stone Hut	4 x 5	Feb. '88	14 x 11	Websters Falls, Greensville
42	Leaves on Moss	4 x 5	Oct. '90	11½ x 8½	Bruce's Caves Conservation Area, Collingwood

CHRONOLOGY
THERESA KAZMIERCZAK-STUBLER

Born

December 8, 1954, Hamilton, Ontario

Solo Exhibits

New Street Gallery, Burlington, Ontario, 1986

Beckett Gallery, Hamilton, Ontario, 1988

The Photo Gallery, Hamilton, Ontario, 1988

Private Exhibition, The Armory, Dundas, Ontario, 1989

Century House Gallery, Caledonia, Ontario, 1990

Awards

Photography Exchange Program with Kaga, Japan, 1989

Publications

Six posters, Artistica, Montreal, 1985

Two posters, Mintmark Press, Toronto, 1988

Lectures and Workshops

One- and two-week workshops in camera and darkroom technique, annually, since 1987

Various lectures at art schools, high schools, colleges and universities.

Designed by Andrew Smith

Typeset in Bodoni and pages composed by Andrew Smith Graphics Inc.

Edited by Dennis Mills

Printed on 100-lb Eco Classic, a re-cycled and acid-free paper from Provincial Papers,
by Herzig Somerville Limited

Bound by The Bryant Press Limited